Museums in the Social and Economic Life of a City

Summary of a Conference
Sponsored by
the American Association of Museums,
Partners for Livable Places, and
the Philadelphia Initiative for Cultural Pluralism

American Association of Museums
1996

"Museums in the Social and Economic Life of a City," a
conference sponsored by the American Association of
Museums, Partners for Livable Places, and the Philadelphia
Initiative for Cultural Pluralism, was held in Philadelphia on
March 4 and 5, 1993.

Summary prepared by:
Keens Company
200 North Little Falls Street
Suite 303
Falls Church, VA 22046
(703) 237-2900
(703) 237-2902 (fax)

Project Director: William Keens
Project Coordinator: Gregory Roby
Project Editor: Reynolds Childress
Project Associates: Debra Braschell and Kenna Simmons

Contents

Day One

Welcome and Introduction

SPEAKERS:

Robert Sorrell, President, Urban League of Philadelphia; Cochair, Philadelphia Initiative for Cultural Pluralism

Hon. Edward G. Rendell, Mayor, Philadelphia

SUMMARY OF REMARKS BY ROBERT SORRELL

Robert Sorrell welcomed the participants to Philadelphia, the city of "brotherly love and sisterly affection." Referring to the dichotomy used by Charles Dickens in *A Tale of Two Cities,* Sorrell described the status of museums in Philadelphia as "the best of times and the worst of times for urban and not-so-urban institutions." He urged the audience to visit such places as the Franklin Institute, the Philadelphia Museum of Art, the Balch Institute for Ethnic Studies, the Afro-American Historical and Cultural Museum, and the Freedom Theatre to see firsthand the "two sides" of the city.

"Museums in the Life of a City: The Philadelphia Initiative for Cultural Pluralism" began in 1989 with funding from the Pew Charitable Trusts and has launched eleven pilot partnerships between cultural institutions and community organizations. The goal of the project, Sorrell explained, is to "build and nurture mutually beneficial relationships." He acknowledged two attendees who were instrumental in the success of that initiative: Portia Hamilton-Sperr, the project director, and Cynthia Primas, the assistant project director.

Sorrell related the goals of the conference: to examine the role of cultural institutions and museums in communities, to explore the diversity of their leadership, and to address their common concerns. He stressed that institutions must be relevant to the constituencies they serve. This is not always easy, especially in a city such as

Philadelphia, which is home to many diverse communities. Indeed, "minority groups" comprise the majority of residents. Learning to recognize and accept diversity within a community, he added, will lead to more "livable" places and institutions that are involved in the community and mutually geared toward sustaining and improving the urban environment.

SUMMARY OF REMARKS BY EDWARD RENDELL

The museums of Philadelphia, lamented Edward Rendell, have generally failed to serve "ordinary" citizens. Many museums in the United States have the reputation, sometimes deserved and sometimes not, of "catering exclusively to wealthier people from prosperous sections of major cities and the suburbs." In Philadelphia, however, the Philadelphia Initiative for Cultural Pluralism is taking steps to help museums overcome that bias. One such project is the "Avenue of the Arts," where approximately nine entertainment venues in a "streetscaped" area will enhance the economic development and the quality of life of the city.

"It is critical," Rendell asserted, "that the offerings of a museum affect the entire community." As an example, he described an outreach program that involves the Philadelphia Museum of Art. Latino college and high school students are trained in the purposes of the museum and the arts and then sent out into their communities as teaching "disciples." He also mentioned the Please Touch Museum in Philadelphia, which involves children in its exhibits. "It is a wonderful sight," he affirmed, "because the children interact with works that widen their scope."

Rendell asserted that museum exhibits must be interactive. Furthermore, museums themselves must be interactive with the communities they do and should serve. "Art enriches life," but that enrichment should not be the "exclusive preserve of people from a particular economic group." Museums that reach out to unserved segments of the population will broaden their base, he argued, and make themselves more self-sustaining—"a noble goal for cultural institutions when public funds are scarce."

Keynote Address

SPEAKER:

Raul Yzaguirre, Chairman, Independent Sector; Executive Director, National Council of La Raza, Washington, DC

SUMMARY OF REMARKS BY RAUL YZAGUIRRE

Raul Yzaguirre voiced his strong support for the conference and the Philadelphia Initiative for Cultural Pluralism. The participants, he claimed, have found an answer to what is "plaguing many cities in the United States," and he congratulated them for not "losing faith." He applauded the wisdom they showed in "uniting museums and other cultural institutions with the economic and social viability of a city."

Yzaguirre admitted that he is a recent convert to that wisdom, which he now zealously embraces. Previously, however, he perceived "culture" as a part of society reserved for the leisure class. He viewed an abstract painting, for example, as an "incomprehensible artwork," with paint randomly splattered on a canvas. And, as he readily acknowledges, with his Spanish accent the word "museum" sounds much like "mausoleum"—a place for "dead people and for statues that serve only as perches for pigeons."

He has since realized the importance of culture. Upper- and middle-class Americans, he stressed, grow up with a well-grounded identity and a sense of their history and direction. But the same is not true for poor people and minority groups, he asserted, who grow up without access to the knowledge that helps them answer the basic questions: "Who are we? Where are we going? What is the meaning of life?" Because of that deficiency, he concluded, it is more important for underserved and disadvantaged groups to understand their culture and history.

If cultural institutions evolve and become relevant to minority communities, they can transform an often negative self-concept into a positive one by instilling in community members confidence and the drive to achieve. "Only if you are well grounded in your identity," he claimed, "can you benefit from an education." One of the fundamental predictors of students' success in school is their belief in their own abilities, which results from being part of an environment that "declares the worth of the individual as well as the individual's role in and contribution to the society."

"Millions of American children," he maintained, "are cut off from their history." Whether they are descended from Germans, Italians, Poles, Africans, or Hispanics, they need "to feel proud about who they are and to know they have a history that is worth learning about." Only then, Yzaguirre argued, can we deal with the ills of urban America. For instance, people do not commit crimes "when they have a positive sense of their identity and when they feel they have a stake in the society."

Fostering cultural pride is more than just a form of "cultural chauvinism," according to Yzaguirre. If people know their own culture and past, then they can relate that knowledge to another person's. "If I understand Aztec pyramids, for example, then I can understand something about Egyptian pyramids." Being aware of "our culture, history, and contribution to society makes us freer and more open to understand and respect other people's. You respect others only if you respect yourself," Yzaguirre concluded, "which is the essence of culture."

War, as the saying goes, is "too important to be left to the generals." In that vein, Yzaguirre maintained, museums and other cultural institutions are "too important to be left to the curators." That, he emphasized, was the focus of the present conference: "If we allow this movement to become a "secret compartment" owned by a select few and if we do not open it to the entire community, then we have lost it. The movement cannot," he insisted, "be for the elite." Each institution, from the parent-teacher association to the city zoning office, must be involved in cultural issues.

Yzaguirre spoke of his involvement in the All-American Cities program, which honors ten American cities each year for their progressive approaches to government and the quality of life. Examining the inner workings of several U.S. cities was highly "educational" for Yzaguirre. Many cities, he noted, "have used culture, museums, festivals, and the arts to renovate neighborhoods." They have reformed and revitalized decaying and blighted areas by anchoring a cultural or educational institution or program in their midst.

Using art and culture to restore a city is not a vague concept, Yzaguirre explained. It is a "proven method," the results of which social scientists can measure by taking surveys on such issues as community pride and by comparing the tourist and entertainment dollars spent in communities. The Clinton administration has frequently discussed the restoration of the infrastructure of American cities, Yzaguirre noted, adding that the concept of "infrastructure" should also include places of art and culture. They are as important to the well-being of a city and its inhabitants as sewers and streets.

Partners for Livable Places, a cosponsor of the present conference, has learned that urban culture and economic development are inextricably linked. Tourists visit the great cities of the world—such as Paris, Rome, and Florence—not so much for the food or the climate, but for the cultural and artistic experience. "Cities like Philadelphia must offer that same attraction."

Any discussion of art and culture, Yzaguirre continued, involves an examination of "why we are here"—a difficult question for practical-minded Americans. But that question "lies at the heart of culture, history, and art, and we need to return to the understanding that what has made other societies cohesive and functional has been a range of aesthetic and spiritual rituals that were taken for granted as a part of daily life." That notion is lost, said Yzaguirre. "We no longer have that anchor of myths and rituals because we have exploded them and have not replaced them. Thus, we will continue to drift as a society unless we grapple with the basic issue of who we are as a people." Yzaguirre urged the participants to be a part of that process of exploration.

QUESTIONS AND ANSWERS

Q: Is there a tension or a contradiction between building a cohesive society and concurrently promoting diversity and multiculturalism?

A: The notion that there is one sterile, homogenized, all-purpose culture for Americans is absurd. We all maintain some distinctiveness, even those of us whose families have lived here for generations. But we can't create a cohesive society by asking people to do away with their differences overnight. And if we allow ethnocentric attitudes to prevail, then we are promoting chauvinism and division. The only alternative is mutual self-respect: understanding one another's cultures and values and rejoicing in that richness and diversity. If we see diversity as a threat, then we are dead as a nation.

As a child, I was unaware of my eighteenth-century Basque heritage, and I was cut off from a knowledge of the civil rights struggles of my ancestors in Texas. I felt like a stranger in my own land. Textbooks told me that what my ancestors brought to this nation was worthless. And if they were worthless, I thought, then I was worthless. That experience is repeated over and over again in the lives of many of our children.

Q: Talking about "meaning" and "value" is often as embarrassing in America as talking about sex. Why are people who bring up such subjects often accused of being "unreal," and the topics dismissed as too esoteric?

A: That is a definite problem. As I travel around the country, however, I find that people are searching for "meaning" and "value," even if they are not using those terms. I do not want to identify myself with secular humanists or antisecular humanists, but there is a sense in this society that if we talk too much about value and meaning, we get dangerously close to religion. We have not found a way to discuss spiritual values without talking about our own personal sense of religion. We must find a new vocabulary so that we can discuss what is important to all of us: the age-old questions of who we are and why we are here. In other societies, those questions are foremost in people's lives.

Q: Museums are in a quandary because they want to deal with vital issues and provide the framework of culture and context, but they are much safer if they deal with objects in a neutral framework. As soon as they venture beyond that, they might be congratulated, but they are exposing themselves to controversy. How can we support and encourage museums to move beyond the realm of "safe"?

A: There is a notion that museums need to focus on eternal and transcendent issues that go beyond the current fads in popular culture. But museums must also be relevant and customer-driven. I am on a task force that is exploring how the Smithsonian Institution should serve the Hispanic population. Its approach *must* be customer-driven. What cultural, artifactual, and museum-oriented desires of the Hispanic community can the Smithsonian fulfill? Curators must not become panderers to current cultural appetites. But if they become aloof from and unconnected to the people they serve, then they become irrelevant. We must find a middle ground between those two extremes.

Q: How can we make culture and the arts as attractive a career or pastime to children as sports, for instance?

A: We must find a way to make the arts and culture as exciting as basketball. We have glamorized the activity of men running around in shorts and throwing a ball through a hoop. We need to use the same technique with culture and the arts. Ascribing prestige and importance

to an activity is something that we already know how to do. If advertisers can market a basketball player on a cereal box, then perhaps they can use that same cereal box to teach the arts and culture. If enough of us banded together to talk to the cereal companies, I suspect they would respond.

Q: In your review of proposals for the All-American Cities program, have any ideas emerged for the resurgence of the Works Progress Administration?

A: Ideas have emerged at the city, state, and federal levels. Projects similar to Civilian Conservation Corps and WPA activities have been sponsored by various funding sources, and the Clinton administration has discussed reinstituting some of those programs. Some of the best art in this country was created during the 1930s and sponsored by the WPA. In public policy, it surprises me how we allow failures to continue and successes to go by the wayside. It is time to resurrect some of those successes.

Building Community/Museum Partnerships

SPEAKERS:

Carmen Febo-San Miguel, President, Board of Directors, Taller Puertorriqueñno, Philadelphia

Cheryl McClenney-Brooker, Vice President of External Affairs, Philadelphia Museum of Art, Philadelphia

Frank Jewell, Executive Director, Valentine Museum, Richmond

Robert C. Bobb, City Manager, Richmond

Kelly Woodland, Coordinator, Career Center, Franklin Institute, Philadelphia

Treopia Washington, Education Program Coordinator, NAACP National Office, Baltimore

---

SUMMARY OF REMARKS BY CARMEN FEBO-SAN MIGUEL

Carmen Febo-San Miguel addressed the importance of collaboration with museums from the perspective of a community organization. His organization, Taller Puertorriqueño, has played a part—as have many African-American, Asian, and other Latino cultural groups—in "raising our voices to object to the monolithic, Eurocentric vision of museums," said Febo San Miguel. "To ignore the diversity in our culture is to continue to ignore the multiplicity of peoples that comprise our country."

Closing one's eyes to these multiple voices and visions condemns art and culture to be rigid and unresponsive. "Unless we are genuinely moved to incorporate these visions, all our artistic solutions will continue to lack meaning for a significant percentage of the population," Febo-San Miguel warned. Within this framework, community organizations such as Taller do not see themselves as isolated institutions but as integral parts of the failures, successes, problems, and solutions of the Latino community. "We create culture, we promote art, we are politically active," said Febo-San Miguel. "And we collaborate when a collaboration is a means to accomplish these goals."

Collaboration is important to Taller because it can provide resources the organization does not have, which in turn benefits the community. Collaboration is also useful for building long-term relationships that can act as bridges between various organizations and communities. Taller is looking for partners who "recognize our expertise, our knowledge of our community, the access we have to our audience, and the knowledge of our art, culture, artists, problems, and solutions," Febo-San Miguel said. When these conditions are met, then collaboration is an opportunity for networking, breaking barriers, providing exposure, exchanging ideas, and expanding and generating funding.

One such collaboration—between Taller Puertorriqueño, the Philadelphia Museum of Art, and the Congreso des Latinos Unidos—took place as part of the Philadelphia Initiative for Cultural Pluralism. The museum's goals included increasing the number and diversity of its audience, expanding programming, promoting cultural pluralism, mentoring youth, and combating cultural alienation. From the perspective of the Congreso des Latinos Unidos, the initiative was an opportunity to advocate the use of its programs and collaborate with Taller and the museum. And Taller wanted to enhance its relationship with the museum, develop a new one with Congreso, expand programs and networking, support local artists, and help museum staff and college students gain a better understanding of Latino culture.

The project involved several phases. First, five college students and five Latino high school interns underwent an eight-week training course at the museum featuring culture sensitivity workshops, crafts projects, and field trips. Once trained, teams of one college student and one intern conducted workshops to translate their experiences into existing programs at Taller and Congreso. In the end, the high school students joined with local artists to create a mural at a middle school that depicted the life of Roberto Clemente, a famous Puerto Rican baseball player for the Pittsburgh Pirates. Febo-San Miguel called the program a success, as it reached more than 2,500 children and visitors through the Department of Recreation, local neighborhood organizations, and summer camps.

The collaboration worked, in Febo-San Miguel's opinion, because the museum sincerely attempted both to build on the expertise of Taller and Congreso and to design the project to meet their needs. "We felt there was an effort to maximize the benefits to the community organizations by thinking of ways the students could benefit from the project, and by leaving something for the community in the form of the mural," he said. "And, because we have been working with the museum on less complicated projects, this additional collaboration was an instrument in developing trust and building on the relationship."

SUMMARY OF REMARKS BY CHERYL MCCLENNEY-BROOKER

Before discussing the Philadelphia Initiative for Cultural Pluralism, Cheryl McClenney-Brooker offered a few remarks on the bargaining process integral to forming partnerships. Referring to the writings of psychologists Morton Deutsch and Robert Krauss, McClenney-Brooker noted their basic definition of a bargain: an agreement between parties settling what each shall give and receive. Deutsch and Krauss elaborate this definition to include tacit, informal agreements as well as formal ones and then apply it to their study of social life. "Well before a community group and museum can enter into consideration of building a partnership, they must participate in the bargaining process," McClenney-Brooker said. "And before the community organization or the museum approaches a negotiation with another entity, it must undergo an internal bargaining procedure."

The Philadelphia Initiative for Cultural Pluralism created just such a forum for bargaining among different racial communities. As one of the authors of the initiative, McClenney-Brooker explained that its goals were to confront and address the racism and prejudice embedded in museums, among both staff and collections. Eleven projects were involved, challenging participants to examine their own prejudices and stereotypes. "Did we honestly confront and erode racism in museums?" McClenney-Brooker asked. "Probably not overtly. But the time invested in the process is likely to be the strongest determinant in getting participants to confront these urgent issues.

For her, the initiative asked the following questions: What is the objective of the bargain? Is it enough for the museum to set a goal of broadening audiences? Is it enough for the community organization to set a goal of exposing individuals to culture through the partner museum? Concluding that the short-term objectives of this bargaining process are meaningful, McClenney-Brooker believes that they are only superficial aspects of new relationships. "When we speak of the long-term objectives of bargaining, the terrain gets rockier." There, the real work begins: addressing questions such as who makes decisions and who has power and translating the answers into jobs, board memberships, and interpretation in the day-to-day functioning of the institution.

Using a proposed study on diversity by the Philadelphia Museum of Art as an example of what can go wrong in the bargaining process, McClenney-Brooker examined some of the mistakes that administrators made in trying to apply the initiative to the museum. The diversity study was intended to look at all aspects of the museum—hiring, board memberships, acquisitions, and audience development. First, the museum brought in a facilitator, but neglected to prepare its staff for the project.

"We had our facilitator make a presentation to the board, and the board did not understand what was going on," McClenney-Brooker recalled. "Needless to say, everyone was ready to throw out the idea."

Although the study did not take place, the museum has established a task force on audience diversity composed of department heads. "These are the people with the real power. They can decide whether such a project happens," she said. Thus, McClenney-Brooker discovered that internal building, brokering, and bargaining are vital prerequisites for getting the study off the ground. It is, however, a time-consuming process. The task force has been at work for almost two years, with more yet to do. But McClenney-Brooker is sure that this effort will succeed. "And we will be better off because we decided to back away and involve the very people who would be integral to making the project work."

The initiative makes clear the need for long-term collaboration, and the museum considers its five-year relationship with Taller Puertorriqueño to be very important in this regard. The museum has now begun taking the next steps in the collaboration, holding planning meetings with Latino leaders to solicit advice about reaching out to the Latino community. The museum's managers and curators have also spent time at Taller, learning more about Latino culture. The long-term arrangement may lead to an exhibition, and McClenney-Brooker hopes staff from both institutions will continue to visit each other.

Who bears the message about diversity can make the difference between a successful project and one that fails. "The more broad the cross section of stakeholders, the less likely that the single vocal proponent will be marginalized," McClenney-Brooker commented. "If museums and community groups can get beyond perceptions of threats involving loss of identity, control, and power and can extend themselves further with limited financial and temporal resources, they may then have the chance to establish a partnership of true equity. If not, then they will wind up with little more than attractive photographs and impressive annual report copy."

SUMMARY OF REMARKS BY FRANK JEWELL AND ROBERT BOBB

Presenting as a team, Frank Jewell, executive director of the Valentine Museum, and Robert Bobb, city manager of Richmond, Virginia, offered a look at the unique partnership between the museum and the city. As a city manager, Bobb's goals are to "latch on to entrepreneurial museum directors" and form partnerships that will lead to economic development and growth, and serve as a marketing tool for economic development activities. What has made the partnership with the Valentine possible, Bobb noted, is the museum's inclusiveness—its mission is to serve all the citizens of Richmond. "The Valentine Museum, from our perspective, is a vehicle for understanding among people," he explained.

It is also a "flourishing economic anchor" and a source of new economic development. Bobb has been able to incorporate the Valentine in a number of projects and uses the museum as a source of expertise. For example, the city is currently trying to establish a visitor's orientation center. "It would have been easy for us to develop the normal sort of facility that merely houses various pamphlets and brochures for tourists," Bobb noted. "When we consulted with the Valentine, however, the orientation center became a veritable theater of exhibits for our city." The city is also relying on the Valentine to help develop an African-American Sports Hall of Fame. "Look to museums as an important and integral part of your overall economic thrust," Bobb urged city administrators and mayors, adding that "the only way this can be successful is if the museum community reaches out to ethnic groups and practices inclusiveness."

From the Valentine's perspective, "if we want to be an effective player in Richmond, we have to have a good working relationship with the city government," said

Jewell. "We have gone out of our way to try and establish that relationship." In fact, the collaboration has been built over a number of years, beginning with the museum's design of a multiscreen presentation for the orientation center. The city also asked the museum to work with an African-American history museum to organize an exhibit about Jackson Ward, an area the city wanted to renovate. The Valentine helped stage a street festival, which has now become an annual event.

Another community program at the Valentine concerns working with at-risk students. Currently, the museum is in the fourth year of a collaborative project with a Johns Hopkins University program for gifted and talented youth. "We noticed when the collaboration began that there were no black students in the program, which struck us as odd," Jewell recalled. "So we worked with Johns Hopkins to integrate the program fully."

The Valentine has also called on Bobb to help with its expansion plans. A corporate gift of land, a building, and cash for renovation got the project rolling, but "the community really wanted some sign that the city was going to back us," Jewell explained. "Bobb went out on a limb for us and came up with $1.2 million, which for Richmond is a significant gift to a private institution."

The museum's principal contact has been through Bobb's office. The Valentine's staff consults Bobb before taking up any action with the city council. In return, the museum tries to respond to Bobb's needs as they arise. This relationship is not, however, about serving any particular elite community, asserted Jewell. "The reason we can be in partnership with the city government is that we work very hard for the whole community."

"It is easy to do museum development if there is an overall tie to some long-term economic development for the city," said Bobb. For example, the Valentine's expansion is part of a $600 million effort by the city to redevelop its riverfront. The museum offered an opportunity to generate visas by 2,000 to 3,000 tourists each year. From an economic development standpoint, that's a very easy

overall economic development strategy. For instance, the street festival in Jackson Ward takes place in an area where the city is engaged in massive redevelopment. The festival brings people into the area, but also connects people with their history and provides an opportunity to develop a vision for the future. "None of this could happen if the museum did not go the extra mile to recognize the diversity of our community," Bobb concluded. "The museum is not seen as an institution only for a particular segment, but is embraced by the entire community. That could only come about as a result of their outreach program, and that makes it easier for me to work through the political process and incorporate their programs as part of our strategy."

SUMMARY OF REMARKS BY KELLY WOODLAND
Kelly Woodland began his discussion of outreach efforts at the Franklin Institute by offering some personal observations on forming partnerships. Rather than reaching out and telling people how great museums are, "I think we have to bring some folks together and allow them to bring the greatness of their community into our museums," he said. Many museum administrators speak of communities as if they were uncharted land: "We have to go into the community." What has not been realized, Woodland said, is that "you cannot go to a place that you are in already. We *are* in the community."

Museums currently "concentrate on the program, not the initiative. A project only runs for the duration of the funding, but the initiative continues." Museums cannot simply come to community organizations when they have the money to do a project. "We sometimes have the perception of community organizations as working in unsophisticated environments on a dirt floor beneath the glow of a twenty-watt bulb," Woodland noted. "We think we are going to shed some light on what they are doing. In turn, they feel that we have money coming out of our ears." Instead, what partners can offer each other is the talent, ingenuity, and ability to make things happen. Forming relationships is the key to successful community-museum communication. Woodland recalled telling the director of education at the Franklin Institute that "working and developing a relationship in the community is not rocket science. And she cut me off and said, 'You know, if it were rocket science it would be a little easier.'"

It may not be rocket science, Woodland continued, but it is a people issue. "Remember the Nike slogan: 'Just Do It,'" he said. "Sometimes at forums like this I feel that we are preaching to the choir. People who need to make the change may not be here."

The specific program Woodland is involved with at the Franklin Institute brought together the Germantown Boys and Girls Club, the National Organization of Black Chemists and Chemical Engineers, and the National Society of Black Engineers. "We had a relationship that started before the money—or the idea—came," he noted. Woodland had already offered meeting space to the two professional organizations, knowing that many of the programs he was interested in involved mentors. He was also familiar with the Germantown community, having grown up there. He brought the organizations together in a program that used science as the catalyst to promote self-esteem, leadership, responsibility, and independence, while also fostering an interest in science itself. "We knew the Franklin Institute does a great job with teacher training and science kits, and we had the resources right there," Woodland explained. "We had another group of resources—the black engineers and chemists. The Germantown Boys and Girls Club provided the young people. On Saturday mornings, twenty-five kids would come to the Franklin Institute and learn about science and engineering from black professional engineers and scientists." Participants from the Boys and Girls Club also had an opportunity to pass along what they learned to younger members of their community.

"This program worked as well as it looked on paper,"

Woodland stated. "I don't think there are too many programs like that." One of the things that made it work was the flexibility of the staff. Using the metaphor of a quarterback calling an audible at the line of scrimmage to change the play at the last minute, Woodland recalled that "sometimes we would go into the room to work with the young people, and we could tell by the looks on their faces that what we had planned was not going to work that day. So we would call an audible and change the plan."

The program met the needs of all parties involved. It gave the engineers and chemists an opportunity to give something back to the community. It gave the Germantown Boys and Girls Club the chance to develop a science program at their community center and to teach younger kids about science. And it gave the Franklin Institute the opportunity to make a difference in the lives of the students. "We enjoyed ourselves, and at the same time we realized that we were getting something done and that the difference could only be made because we had formed this partnership. We all got together and we 'just did it.'"

SUMMARY OF REMARKS BY TREOPIA WASHINGTON

Currently serving as education program coordinator for the NMCP, Treopia Washington was previously codirector for the Community Group Partnership Program at the Association of Science-Technology Centers (ASTC). The association includes science museums, zoos, aquariums, botanical gardens, and children's museums and has been involved in outreach programs and partnerships since 1986. In 1990, ASTC conducted a survey entitled *A Status Report on the Role of Minorities, Women, and People with Disabilities in Science Centers*. Washington explained that the survey included the following recommendations for museum directors:

• Strengthen ties to key leaders in underserved communities—elected officials, religious leaders, university faculty, and community activists. Acquaint them with the institution and share its goals.

• Develop an advisory board composed of community leaders and museum board members to come up with an action plan for the museum.

• Conduct informal surveys on how the museum is serving a newly targeted audience. Count how many minority, female, and disabled visitors the museum attracts at a given time.

• Stress to museum staff that diversifying the audience is a priority. Let floor staff know that welcoming all visitors is an important part of their job.

• Increase recruitment and training for minority, female, and disabled staff members.

Recommendations for museum staff included:

• Notice who comes to the museum and whether they come as individuals or members of groups. Count the minority, female, and disabled visitors to the museum.

• Be aware of your own behavior toward visitors. Ask yourself whether you are equally helpful to all visitors.

• Learn about other communities. Expand your knowledge of others by reading publications targeted at social and cultural groups other than your own.

Washington, through her work with the Community Group Partnership Program, has been able to see the importance of the above recommendations while developing some insights of her own. Early on, she realized that museum-community relationships are not established quickly and must be allowed to develop over time. For example, some six years ago she discovered that many families from "disadvantaged" areas who did not have easy access to museums had never visited a museum specializing in science. At an annual conference for Title

I parents, Washington "took a risk" and initiated a visit to a local science museum for the parents who accompanied her to the conference. That visit was so successful that Washington now organizes a new museum visit around every Title I conference. More and more parents call her weeks in advance wondering which museum they are going to tour.

Museums must engender a sensitivity to the communities they serve, asserted Washington. She offered the example of a museum director who complained, at one of a series of meetings convened to introduce museum staffs to local community leaders, that few members of the surrounding African-American community ever visited his museum. A local resident informed him that the museum was located adjacent to a shopping center that made locals feel uncomfortable because some people associated with the center had been "unfriendly" to them. This sort of information is necessary stressed Washington for museums to work successfully with their communities.

Frequently, museums do more harm than good when they try to include target groups through "one-shot deals." Washington urged participants to include target groups throughout the year. "It is not so much the exhibits or the activities that are important. The most important thing is helping people feel welcome by assuring them that they are a valuable part of the entire operation."

In closing, Washington listed what she calls the "three C's" necessary for change:

• *Commitment.* Obstacles are not always overcome on the first attempt. If one plan does not work, try another.

• *Caring.* "If you don't care, people can tell."

• *Cooperation.* Everyone has something to contribute; when everyone is contributing, both museums and communities grow and improve.

Luncheon Video Presentation

SPEAKER:

Courtenay Cannady, Independent Consultant, Johnson Homes Tenant Council, Philadelphia

---

SUMMARY OF REMARKS BY COURTENAY CANNADY

As a public relations consultant, Courtenay Cannady worked with the James Weldon Johnson Homes public housing development, which was the first such development constructed in Philadelphia. She has nurtured not only a working relationship with the residents, but also a strong friendship that transcends the "walls of public housing."

Cannady was the director of the Johnson Homes Oral History Video Project, which produced a video entitled *Spaces of the Heart.* The development, she noted, has the "same goals and aspirations as other communities and has a history and culture that are important to preserve and share." The Philadelphia Initiative for Cultural Pluralism has been vital in those processes because it has empowered the residents to "tell their story," which would otherwise never have been heard outside the community.

Both the residents and the surrounding community benefited from the project, said Cannady. The residents developed research, interviewing, and video production skills, thus improving their self-image and enhancing their opportunities for employment. The Free Library experienced increased use of its facility by people who had previously felt alienated from their community.

The "tale" residents told began before and continues beyond the *Spaces of the Heart* video. Cannady pointed out that public housing began as William Penn's ideal of a "utopian country town." In the modern era, the community public housing project developed numerous problems. Now, however, through the aid of such programs as the Philadelphia Initiative for Cultural Pluralism, residents are taking the lead in transforming their developments into the "ideal of public housing."

The Caring Community: Social Problems and Cultural Institutions

MODERATOR:

John Tenhula, President, Balch Institute of Ethnic Studies, Philadelphia

PANELISTS:

Luis Cancel, Commissioner of the Arts, New York City

Sister Mary Scullion, Project Home, Philadelphia

Peter Sterling, President, Indianapolis Children's Museum, Indianapolis

Lily Yeh, Artist; Founder and Executive Director, Village of Arts and Humanities, Philadelphia

Shane Smith, Executive Director, Cheyenne Botanic Gardens, Cheyenne, Wyoming

Nancy Darmstadter, Assistant Director for Education, Academy of Natural Sciences, Philadelphia

SUMMARY OF REMARKS BY JOHN TENHULA

Moderator John Tenhula began by establishing a point of commonality among those present: "We are all caring, or we would not be in our jobs doing what we are doing." There are, of course, many ways a community can show it cares. Thus, Tenhula explained, the speakers to follow would discuss "the jobs they are doing by relating specific programs established at their institutions" and how these programs tackle local problems.

Tenhula referred to several issues addressed in the American Association of Museums' report, *Excellence and Equity: Education and the Public Dimension of Museums,* that were also likely to be raised in the session:

education, making diversity work, creating and promoting learning opportunities, respecting cultures and intellectual perspectives, and committing leadership and financial resources to strengthen the public dimension of museums. "I see any partnership as an anthropological process," Tenhula stated. "We all go out there and look at the little villages we live in."

Tenhula ended with two quotes that he hoped would frame the session. The first was from Plato: "The soul takes nothing with her to the other world but her education and her culture." The second was from a seventh-grader who, after visiting the Balch Institute, asked, "What good is this institute if it can't help my neighborhood, or my life, become better?"

SUMMARY OF REMARKS BY LUIS CANCEL

Before becoming New York City's commissioner of the arts, Luis Cancel was director of the Bronx Museum of the Arts. "My career has been shaped through my experiences in building a museum in a community devoid of major resources," Cancel said.

"Having concluded a long time ago that museums have important roles to play in their communities," Cancel remarked that he has never worried that a museum's primary mission of preserving and interpreting its collection would be impaired if the institution also took pains to address the social problems facing its community. In fact, quite the opposite can occur. "If a museum links up with other community-based groups, it is viewed as an integral part of the society. This can translate into additional support for the museum's core mission through improved fund raising and greater public sector support." By embracing its community, a museum is helping to achieve the goal of preserving its collections and fulfilling its educational mission.

In structuring a partnership, the most important thing is to "pick a problem that is affecting your community and somehow intersects with your programmatic mission," Cancel said. He used specific examples from the Bronx Museum to illustrate his point. In 1979, he recalled, the Bronx was the focus of intense media attention as America's symbol for urban blight. While the problems were severe, many community groups, neighborhood organizations, and block associations were trying to rebuild the community. The museum designed an exhibition that "put the problem on a longer time scale," documenting not only the devastation in the Bronx but also efforts to rebuild. Urban planners, architectural historians, sociologists, photographers, and community groups were included in the process. The exhibition helped put the museum on the map, but it also had an effect on the creation and direction of the South Bronx development office.

A second example involved the location of a permanent home for the museum itself on the Grand Concourse (a major thoroughfare) in 1982. The concourse also had the greatest concentration of residential Art Deco architecture in New York City, though it had fallen on hard times. "We had an urban asset that was withering away, but people felt a great sense of pride in it," said Cancel. The museum realized that unless it addressed the larger problem of the concourse itself, it would have trouble attracting visitors to the new facility. Their solution was to create the Committee to Make the Concourse Grand Again and to house the organization right in the museum. "We made a great effort, and spent actual museum resources, launching this group," Cancel recalled. Among the committee's projects were bulk plantings in old flower beds, attempts to combat graffiti, and organizing an annual arts festival. "There was a meshing of the museum's goal—to establish a permanent home—and the need to positively affect the surrounding community," said Cancel. "The fact that the museum and its trustees were involved got noticed. That was part of the reason why the museum was successful in getting the public sector to provide a lot of the capital dollars for renovation."

Yet another example comes from the Brooklyn Children's Museum, which is located in the racially troubled neighborhood of Crown Heights. The museum brought together children from the Hasidic and African-Caribbean communities to learn about their respective cultures and to undertake art projects together. The museum has been viewed as "neutral safe ground where some dialogue can take place," Cancel explained. "The dialogue is not always nice. But it is essential." In Cancel's view, "one of the most important areas where we can take a leadership role is in using the arts to promote understanding and greater tolerance for differences in our society."

SUMMARY OF REMARKS BY SISTER MARY SCULLION

Sister Mary Scullion works with Project Home, a not-for-profit organization focusing on the chronically homeless of Philadelphia. "These people are often stereotyped as panhandlers or mentally ill," said Scullion. To improve their lives, those barriers and stereotypes have to be remediated. (One way the organization confronted these stereotypes was by producing a calendar that combined shots of homeless people with their own writings.)

There is a similar feeling among those who work with the homeless and those who work in museums: both groups feel isolated. To overcome that problem, Project Home began to work with the children in its own neighborhood, asking Lily Yeh, for example, to develop arts and cultural activities. "The children in some of the low-income neighborhoods do not have much opportunity to develop their potential," said Scullion. With the program's success, however, "they have begun to develop their knowledge and skills."

The term "cultural institution" means more to Scullion than merely "the arts." It includes religious and educational organizations, and the family as well. The breakdown of these cultural institutions "has put many of the people I work with on the street, she added. She defined one of the purposes of culture as "promoting the truth"; truth is found in the community at large, where there is a rich, untapped knowledge base. It is vital that cultural institutions explore this base, for, "until it is tapped, what we have to offer will be narrow," remarked Scullion.

Scullion urged cultural institutions to "seize the role of resistance against the dehumanizing elements in our society." Culture is an invaluable resource but can itself become limiting when institutionalized. Because the truth is always dynamic, said Scullion, cultural leaders must encourage critical thinking, among both themselves and others. They must "go out and speak out." Through such leadership, institutions can even be peacemakers. "I do not mean that in any rosy way," Scullion explained. "They have the opportunity to initiate thought about problems and find expressions of peace, harmony, and inclusiveness." By giving expression to "the most fundamental truths of who we all are," cultural institutions can unite communities. Quoting Virginia Woolf on making "unity out of multiplicity," Scullion concluded by noting that this is the challenge museums and other cultural institutions face.

SUMMARY OF REMARKS BY PETER STERLING

Noting that cultural organizations are places of learning and teaching, Peter Sterling laid out their two possible futures: (1) Within ten years, cultural institutions will be central to our culture because other institutions will be in a state of desperation. Or, (2) cultural organizations will be marginalized and unable to maintain the resources they need to continue operating. "We are either going to win dramatically by the end of the decade, or lose terribly.

When the Indianapolis Children's Museum decided to become "an agent of change in the community," it focused on a truly underserved audience: teenagers. There exists age discrimination against teenagers,

Sterling noted. Museums rarely work with them, even though this age group comprises as much as 25 percent of their audience. Furthermore, Sterling pointed out the international importance of focusing on teenagers: Although they are a minority population in the "aging" United States, they are part of a burgeoning worldwide youth population that is increasingly interconnected across geographic boundaries by electronic and print media.

The museum wanted to attract young people "who were going to make a long-term investment in us as we made a long-term investment in them," Sterling explained. Museum staff thus focused on three teenage groups: the "missing in action," who have been abandoned by adults and are likely to drop out of high school; the "watchers, who believe satisfaction is derived from watching other people's accomplishments (usually on television); and the "questers," who want to do something but lack facilities and resources. "Every one of these groups has gifted and talented youngsters who would be an asset to and benefit from the museum," Sterling remarked.

The museum had three goals: First, it wanted to engage these young people. "Margaret Mead once said that youngsters have to have places where adults like them," Sterling noted. "If we did nothing besides that, maybe we could develop a relationship with these young people." In fact, the single most important factor in the relationship between the "missing in action" group and the museum was the fact that an adult there cared about them. Second, the museum wanted to empower young people so that "they could begin to believe in themselves not as viewers and watchers, but as actual doers." The third objective was creating a sense of continuing community service; "if a person had been in the program for three months, he or she would spend some time with a youngster who had only been in it for three days."

To be successful, the museum had to offer activities that young people thought were legitimate. The first step was to dedicate a space in the museum for those 10 and older. Five high school seniors were hired to design the space, and participants in the program were asked what kinds of activity they wanted. They chose the challenging project of expressing worldwide concern over the environment—"not what I would have picked for the first project!" Sterling admitted. The museum staff had to alter its approach to working with these youths. To achieve their goals, the adults had to change from a curatorial stance to one of mentoring or coaching. This change allowed them to develop an apprentice system in which the adults and youth became partners.

The program now has about 500 young people involved, and they have become the program's best salespeople. "There is nothing you can do in normal advertising promotion that will touch a young person as much as their friends asking them to come to the museum," Sterling noted. The program has had the added benefit of introducing participants "to the adult world of work" and the skills it requires to build consensus and make decisions. Said Sterling, "They learn where power lies. More importantly, they find out where wisdom lies. I think they found wisdom in places they never expected to find it: among their friends, inside themselves, and among adults."

In conclusion, Sterling listed several ingredients for a similarly successful program: First, a museum must take a long-term view. Second, trusting, personal relationships must be built between staff and participants. "The word 'caring' is really important," Sterling said. "For many of these adolescents, finding that adults really do care about them is the most significant thing that has happened to them in their lives." Finally, legitimate tasks must be developed for the young people the museum is trying to attract.

SUMMARY OF REMARKS BY LILY YEH

Lily Yeh described the Village of the Arts and Humanities, a community art project she began in 1986. The project was spontaneous from the start. "There was this empty lot," Yeh recalled. "Naively I said, 'I am going to build a park.'" Armed with a $2,500 grant from the Pennsylvania Council for the Arts, she began to involve community youth in building a new space in an otherwise neglected neighborhood.

Traditionally, there has been much tension in Yeh's North Philadelphia community between Korean merchants and African Americans. Yeh remembers being told that teenagers in the neighborhood would destroy whatever she built. "I said, 'Wow, those are the very people I must recruit to help me build the park,'" she recalled. For three summers, children were her only volunteers, helping her make sculptures. Eventually, drawn by the children, adults joined in the work.

Yeh described the project as "organic." It is not permanent. There are no preconceived ideas, no preliminary designs. For instance, she wanted a fence to provide a boundary and create a sense of order, but not a fence that said "Keep Out." In 1989, she asked some local adults—mostly parents, many with drug problems—to join the project and help create the fence. After setting up a boundary fence, their input grew until they had turned one empty lot into a flower garden and another into a community vegetable garden. The village later inherited a building, and this allowed Yeh and her cohorts to create other programs, such as a cooking class. The project began to host artists as well, offering free art workshops to neighborhood residents.

The project at the village, Yeh said, "is really about using art projects to build communities. The art project must be big, significant, challenging, and risky. Through the building of the park, we began to build our community. The world today seems to pay attention only to high-tech projects. But the village is about low-tech. Just with the pair of hands we were born with, we ought to be able to do something." And being impermanent, the village should change with the times and the community: "When it outlasts its function, it should be replaced."

SUMMARY OF REMARKS BY SHANE SMITH
The Cheyenne Botanic Garden is the only such garden in the country that sets social work as its chief priority, noted Shane Smith. It is also one of the nation's smallest municipal gardens, with only about 6,800 square feet of solar-heated conservatory. The organization works with three usually marginalized groups, which it calls "client volunteers": senior citizens, at-risk youth, and the handicapped. This combination reflects a different sort of cultural diversity than that found in East Coast cities, said Smith, and hence is quite unique.

These groups make up the garden's main labor force, providing upwards of 95 percent of the labor, much more than is usually provided by such volunteer forces. Smith attributes this high percentage to the fact that most involved see it as "horticultural therapy." Seniors, for instance, much prefer beautifying the gardens to playing bridge or taking aerobics. Clients in general gain a sense of self-esteem through the meaningful labor of planting and harvesting, through helping a wilted plant regain its strength. Moreover, horticulture is an activity that can be adjusted to different levels of ability. People with poor motor coordination or mental disabilities find they can contribute as much as anyone. Another benefit: "The socializing is great for many of our clients."

Smith credited the diversity of the targeted groups with making the project work. And just as importantly, their contributions have enabled the facility to survive the threat of decreased budgets. "There is nothing like a bunch of senior citizens dressed in green, packing a city council hall when we are about to get our budget cut," he noted. "All of a sudden, we get a unanimous vote to keep the funding." Furthermore, the garden provides 40,000 bedding plants to the city for beautification efforts. "We have been able to sell it to local politicians as an investment in tourism, as a social project, as a senior citizen, youth, and handicapped workshop area, and as a place of meaningful work." In return, the city gets a botanical garden it probably could not afford otherwise. Thus, "it is an easy project to sell politically."

SUMMARY OF REMARKS BY NANCY DARMSTADTER
Nancy Darmstadter focused her remarks on WINS (Women in Natural Sciences), a program run by Philadelphia's Academy of Natural Sciences for ninth- and tenth-grade girls who are from single-parent homes, have financial need, and have an aptitude in science. WINS has five goals: providing science content, science skills, cooperation and empowerment, environmental stewardship, and access to careers in science. In order to participate, students must fill out an extensive application form and go to the museum for an interview. Darmstadter remarked that the museum sends duplicate materials to the schools where the girls are enrolled, because counselors and teachers often provide as much support as parents. The program begins in the summer by focusing on the theme of "People and the Environment." The girls study endangered species, hear from guest speakers, learn how to read maps, and go on field trips. There is an overnight safari at the academy's museumn where classes are held and the girls and their counselors spend the night. The summer concludes with a week-long camping trip to the Poconos. Fall covers terrestrial ecology; winter, taxonomy and animal classification. In addition, we spend a lot of time behind the scenes in our scientific departments, such as ichthyology and entomology," Darmstadter said. The year concludes with aquatic ecology and a weekend camping trip to Assateague Island National Seashore.

The program also teaches responsibility. As Darmstadter explained, "We teach them to phone if they are not going to be able to attend class. We prepare them for interviews—how to dress, how to be on time." She maintains constant contact with the students and their families throughout the year. The impact of "having a personal relationship with a student day after day is profound," she added.

Students also volunteer in the museum's live animal unit, work as guides for the overnight safari program, and volunteer at the children's nature museum. Beyond the WINS program, many students have begun to work for pay after school at the museum. Funding from the National Science Foundation has allowed the Academy to offer internships, and the program has placed students as interpreters at the Franklin Institute's women in science exhibit, for example, and at the Fairmont Ranger Corps.

The program, said Darmstadter, has changed her life profoundly, not to mention the lives of the girls who have participated. Recalling a friend's comment that networking was the most important factor in motivating at-risk students, Darmstadter explained that the more people one knows in the community, the more likely one can place these students in other institutions, which will continue to nurture them year after year. "The options for these students are limitless," Darmstadter concluded. "They start to see themselves in the context of an institution like the academy. It becomes comfortable, an extension of their neighborhood. I see them go into new situations with much less fear, much more enthusiasm, more self-confidence, and confidence in their ability to become part of society at these institutions."

QUESTIONS AND ANSWERS

Q: Do any of you have a way to track success rates over time?

Sterling: We hired the Center for Evaluation at Indiana University to do a longitudinal study. I will tell you one story that has impressed me: I went to the fiftieth anniversary of the museum of Science and Industry in Chicago. They had invited Nobel laureates from around the world, and every one of them said they had cut their teeth in a museum. Tracking these youngsters longitudinally is possible, but we must be careful not to get caught up in the same conundrum as the schools—the demand by society to have testing, to prove that something has been learned. The biggest change that occurs in our program is attitudinal, in the kids' perceptions of themselves. They can testify to that in as many ways as you would like. They begin to perceive that change in themselves, and they can talk about it.

Darmstadter: When the Johnson Pharmaceutical Company gave us a grant for evaluation, they asked for permission to track our students. They were interested in the success of the program they were funding. So, though our initial funding source was not able to give us money for evaluation or tracking, Johnson is providing those records for us.

Q: How do you rate "caring" in terms of making things happen in a community?

Cancel: That is a resource from which you derive the energy to take on what seems to be an almost insurmountable task. For instance, take Lily's example of getting only $2,500 to rehabilitate an abandoned lot. If you did not have the ability to feel engaged in that attempt, it would seem an impossible task. Clearly, what enabled her to engage the community and stretch the resources was caring. Without the caring, the real engagement by the museum or the change agent, you are not going to succeed.

Yeh: Right now there is a buzz phrase, "Art for social change." Maybe art does not change society. But the heart does. If the heart is hard, it does not make any difference. The program will not change people or build community. But if it comes from a spirit of generosity, something happens.

Sterling: Somebody made the remark that a thousand points of light need batteries. I think the batteries, in this instance, are our human capacity. That is what we have lacked in a lot of these situations: We have had the talk, the rhetoric, without the batteries. That is what we can supply.

Cultural Institutions and Multiculturalism

MODERATOR:

Eduardo Diaz, Director of Arts and Cultural Affairs, San Antonio, Texas

SPEAKERS:

Elaine Vaughn, Outreach Manager, Please Touch Museum, Philadelphia

Kau Our, Human Relations Representative, Philadelphia Commission on Human Relations, Philadelphia

Ronnie Nichols, Director, Delta Cultural Center, Helena, Arkansas

Josey Stamm, Director of Development, University of the Arts, Philadelphia

---

SUMMARY OF REMARKS BY EDUARDO DIAZ

Eduardo Diaz defined culture as the arts, beliefs, customs, institutions, and all products of human work and thought created by a people at a particular time. Museums are institutions devoted to the procurement, care, custody, and display of objects of lasting interest or value. "Putting 'multi' in front of 'culture' and then adding it to 'museum' ought to give museum professionals and supporters some food for thought," he noted.

Examining the "dramatic demographic changes in an emerging new American order," Diaz concluded that two things are occurring: First, established arts institutions are nervous because they do not quite know how to respond to these changes. Second, a new set of aesthetic considerations, expectations, and challenges is being created. In this new order, every culture is important and integral to a community. "It is no mystery why ethnic art continues to grow in popularity," said Diaz. "It reflects the authentic notion of what it is, after all, to be American." Every culture is important to a city, and "responsible municipal leadership needs to acknowledge this set of facts, understand this power, respect and enjoy the diversity, and plan and act accordingly."

The role of museums thus becomes critically important. If every cultural experience and expression deserves support, the question then becomes one of resource allocation within each institution. "How will you work to acknowledge the multiplicity of cultures in your community and give these cultures an opportunity for authentic expression through the exhibition and interpretive activities of your organization?" Diaz asked. He drew a distinction between the democratization of culture—integrating cultural institutions through affirmative action—and cultural democracy—enabling culturally specific centers and projects (including museum-based projects) to develop and thrive while addressing a range of artistic, social, and economic issues. Quoting Gerald Yoshitomi, executive director of the Japanese-American Cultural and Community Center in Los Angeles, Diaz explained that "the democratization of culture requires only that we understand the common support system. Cultural democracy requires each of us to try to understand one another's systems of cultural support. It also requires the trust to believe that cultural groups developing their own cultures under the protection of a separate subsystem will choose to share their culture with others."

Noting the changes in attitude toward the arts (and toward the National Endowment for the Arts, in particular), Diaz concluded that "while we all fight the good fight in Washington, at the state level and at city hall, it is important to redouble our efforts to welcome new images and new audiences of multicultural origins. Museums must affirm multicultural patrimony and project it authentically."

SUMMARY OF REMARKS BY ELAINE VAUGHN

A former social worker, Elaine Vaughn made the jump to museum work three years ago. Yet, as outreach manager for the Please Touch Museum, she finds herself still engaged in working with families in a program designed to draw in new audiences. When she began, Vaughn's mandate was to locate two minority organizations in Philadelphia and set up outreach programs with them using the museum's "traveling trunks." It was not an easy task to get those traditionally left out of the world of cultural institutions to open up to her as that world's representative. She was frequently viewed with distrust, even though she was the product of one of the two communities she engaged.

Vaughn presented to community parents the material the museum had to offer and modeled certain types of behavior—specifically, how parents could interact with their children "in a way to which they are not accustomed." These were families who did not visit museums and who found the idea intimidating—people who "are limited in terms of their education and social skills, isolated in their communities, and do not think of coming to the Please Touch Museum, located in an upscale neighborhood, surrounded by the white middle class."

Vaughn took her trunks into community centers and played with those moms and showed them how to play with their children." She invited them to the museum for free visits. At the end of a three-month period, depending on how often particular parents came to site programs, she offered them a one-year free membership. Vaughn was personal with them when they came to the museum, "letting it embrace them." The first year of the program saw a 30 percent success rate at both sites; the next year, Vaughn visited six sites. At the end of 1992, the number was up to thirty-two. "I do not discriminate," Vaughn noted. "I will go into a residential drug rehab center where I have a locked-in audience. Or I will go to the neighborhood parenting program where parents come voluntarily."

Working with young children makes the museum unique, said Vaughn, because "we have got them when they are like little sponges." Once parents and children know it is okay to come to the Please Touch Museum, as the children grow older, they feel comfortable moving on to the Franklin Institute or the Philadelphia Library. Parents are not embarrassed because "they do not know a particular artifact comes from a particular place, or that a particular painting was done by a particular artist," Vaughn said. Welcoming these parents and children to the museum fosters the idea that it is a place to learn. And Vaughn believes a love of art can grow if children are introduced at a young age to a museum "where there is a multicultural staff, where people are sensitive to families from different walks of life, where everybody is welcome."

"The community," Vaughn concluded, "is what it is all about. If there wasn't a community, there would be no Please Touch Museum."

SUMMARY OF REMARKS BY KAU OUR

A survivor of Cambodia's Khmer Rouge regime, Kau Our immigrated to the United States with his family after the Vietnamese invasion in 1979. Having watched the Khmer Rouge attempt to eradicate Cambodian culture, Our is now trying to preserve his heritage in a country where Cambodians are a small minority. "In Cambodia, we are the majority," Our said. "Here we have to learn a new culture. I have nowhere else to go; I have to be here, and I have to learn from all of you. And I would like to share my culture with you."

Cambodians, Our noted, are proud of their ancestral cultural heritage, passing it down from generation to generation even in the most difficult of circumstances. To continue that practice, the Cambodian community in Philadelphia has formed an association to preserve its art and dance, and especially to teach its children. A language class is offered, for instance, because "we do not want them to forget their relatives left behind in Cambodia. It is important that the children write to them."

Another of the association's efforts involves a dance apprenticeship, featuring a Cambodian dance group that performs throughout Philadelphia. Funding is always tenuous (the program was funded as a pilot, but the money is no longer available), and, like the language class, the dance group depends on volunteers who are sometimes paid and sometimes not. "We do it because we want to display our culture to others," explained Our. Ultimately, he would like to establish a Cambodian cultural center, a place where his fellow Cambodian nationals could exhibit artwork depicting their country's history. The center would thus be both expressive and educational, because, said Our, "a picture can mean many things."

SUMMARY OF REMARKS BY RONNIE NICHOLS

Ronnie Nichols related the story behind the birth of the Delta Cultural Center in Helena, Arkansas. Every October some 70,000 people come to the 1,500-resident town to attend the Helena Blues Festival. Several years ago, at the behest of then-governor Bill Clinton, local residents and legislators took up consideration of an institution to celebrate the region around Helena. When local leaders and festival organizers conceived of a blues museum, Clinton encouraged them to "think bigger"—and the center was born.

For Nichols, the center is an opportunity to draw together the disparate populations of the Delta—white and black, but also Swiss, German, Jewish, and Asian. "A lot of people believe Ellis Island was the only port of entry for immigrants entering this country," Nichols noted. "They do not realize that foreign peoples came up the Mississippi River from New Orleans." An exhibition at the center, "A Land Promised," addresses the many immigrant populations that have come to the Delta.

A recent project at the center, funded by the National Endowment for the Humanities and aimed at reaching underserved communities, involves a mural to be painted by kindergarten-aged children who are teamed up with the elderly. Put a child with an older person, Nichols noted, and they will share all kinds of information. "These are the efforts we are trying to put forth—not just to talk about blues, but to talk about the people of the Delta and who they are, to allow them to rediscover themselves in a region that has been taught to be polarized," Nichols said. "We must understand that we all share some common interests and common bonds."

SUMMARY OF REMARKS BY JOSEY STAMM

For Josey Stamm, multiculturalism is "an intellectual imperative—it is vital to appreciate the enormous enrichment provided by studying diverse human reactions and solutions to the common issues of living." Cultural institutions such as museums can help people become human Rosetta Stones through the presentation of works placed in cultural contexts, "to try to help people understand the work as would a member of the culture being represented."

Stamm's own work involves two major projects devoted to multiculturalism: Festival Mythos and the University of the Arts Alliance. The original idea for Festival Mythos was a small festival devoted to folklore and myth that would bring ten or twelve nationally known artists to Philadelphia. Beyond that, organizers began to consider how they could "ignite a linkage and an exchange where people could participate in understanding and linking diverse belief systems." The search for linkages resulted in a collaboration of eighty-one organizations and numerous "satellites." For example, the University of the Arts commissioned the Village of the Arts and Humanities to create a theater piece based on the stories of the people who are building the park; that piece turned into a collaboration between the village and Venture Theater, a small performing group.

The alliance project, an ongoing partnership between six community organizations and the university, is intended to find ways to strengthen financially all the partners and to enrich them all both educationally and artistically. One result has been extending the collaboration with the Village of the Arts and Humanities, this time on a new theater piece based on Peter Brook's version of the *Mahabharata*. "It occurred to us that this would provide an opportunity to teach almost everything about the arts in one experience," Stamm explained. The project, employing "horticulture, building renovation, mask-making, storytelling, dance, and voice," will take place over three years, with one of the three acts of the *Mahabharata* being performed each summer at the village and at the university.

Audience exchange is also an important part of the alliance. For instance, one of the theaters managed by the university has become the setting for a children's recital by the Point Breeze Performing Arts Center. "The first time that happened, enrollment at Point Breeze increased by 100 percent," Stamm recalled. "The second time, enrollment quadrupled." The alliance is also working to build a new arts center for Point Breeze and is looking into the possibility of building a shopping center that could help support it.

Stamm concluded by noting that through Festival Mythos, she had discovered what "an extraordinary city Philadelphia is for the arts." In addition, "we discovered the strength of community organizations, our own energy, and an ability to collaborate that has carried over into other projects."

Day Two

Welcome and Introduction

SPEAKERS:

Portia Hamilton-Sperr, Director, Philadelphia Initiative for Cultural Pluralism, Philadelphia

Isaac Maefield, Artist, Philadelphia

SUMMARY OF REMARKS BY PORTIA HAMILTON-SPERR

Portia Hamilton-Sperr reviewed the previous day's activities, observing that the call for "truth, values, and inclusion" as well as the need to nurture "cultural identity and cultural democracy" characterized the presentations. The speakers identified two elements critical to a successful museum/community partnership: effective bargaining techniques and sustained financial support. In addition, the presenters expressed their heartfelt commitment to their projects, which they believe in uncompromisingly. Pragmatism must accompany that personal conviction, she cautioned, to achieve a project's mission. One of the goals of the Philadelphia Initiative for Cultural Pluralism, noted Hamilton-Sperr, is for community representatives and museum professionals to "share the responsibilities of the decision-making process," a criterion that points to the necessary "equality" of the partners. That combination, she maintained, drives a successful project.

SUMMARY OF REMARKS BY ISAAC MAEFIELD

"Explorations," the community initiative involving the Parkside Association of Philadelphia and the Philadelphia Maritime Museum, examined how waterways are vital to the life of a city and how they link people and cultures from around the world. Isaac Maefield explained that the program included such activities as a cruise along the Delaware River on the pleasure ship Spirit of Philadelphia, as well as weekly workshops that combined art projects and maritime lore. Workshop leaders encouraged community children to create masks, jewelry, wood sculpture, and clay ships."

At the conclusion of the project, noted Maefield, the Maritime Museum held an exhibition of the children's artworks. In addition, the project documented its efforts via photographs and a video. Documentation of this sort, he stressed, is necessary for preserving the conditions and accomplishments of an initiative.

Maefield acknowledged that Bill Ward, the education director of the museum, brought a "strong multicultural perspective" to the project. Although maritime history traditionally emphasizes the European galleons of the fifteenth and sixteenth centuries, said Maefield, the participants learned that Africa also made a significant contribution during the age of exploration—a "refreshing revelation."

Maefield stressed the need to promote multiculturalism. The multicultural approach to education will help combat racism, which Maefield called the number one mental health problem in our country." Art, which is the driving force behind museums and other cultural institutions, is the primary tool for such social change. "Advocates will undoubtedly confront adversity as they struggle to serve their communities, and so the process demands unwavering commitment. They may feel the need to "cut themselves off from other people, places, and things" to achieve their mission as administrators, educators, and community organizers, warned Maefield, "but we must overcome our differences and unite."

Financing Community/Cultural Institution Partnerships

SPEAKERS:

Sondra Myers, Cultural Adviser to the Governor, Harrisburg, Pennsylvania

Chris Allen, Manager, Community Assistance Program, Arkansas Power and Light Co., Little Rock

Warren Merrick, Development Director, Freedom Theatre, Philadelphia

William Bondurant, Former Executive Director, Mary Reynolds Babcock Foundation, Winston-Salem, North Carolina

---

SUMMARY OF REMARKS BY SONDRA MYERS

Sondra Myers offered her "observations, hopes, and hunches" on the financing of community/cultural institution partnerships. In a time of "economic deficit and social dysfunction," it makes sense to develop new strategies for the support of culture by showing culture's "necessary connection" to community. "Cultural institutions, along with their collections, education departments, and all their intellectual resources, are underused," she asserted. At the same time, they are surrounded by underserved populations. It is not enough "to dwell only on the economic survival" of an institution. Institutional advocates must also show how these institutions benefit the community.

Taking the "high road," she suggested that museum supporters make the environmental case for culture—as an "ecological imperative that must be employed in the whole process of restoring or creating a new, genuine sense of well-being in our communities." Collaboration between cultural institutions and community organizations should be advocated as a primary solution to social needs. "Excellence, yes," said Myers, "not, however, for its own sake, but for the sake of society." She agreed strongly with Congressman Pat Williams's comparison of the plight of the National Endowment for the Arts (NEA) with that of the spotted owl: "It's not about the spotted owl, it's about the habitat. And it's not about the NEA, it's about society."

A report commissioned by the Baltimore Community Foundation, *Building Community: The Arts in Baltimore Together,* addresses the environmental issue in specific ways. Asking questions such as: "How does a community sustain a rich and varied cultural tradition through difficult economic times?" and "How does it strengthen older institutions, encourage new ones, and continue to attract new talent?" the report's authors made six recommendations:

• *Ratify the commitment.* Civic leaders should affirm the place of the arts in the building of community and expand governmental advocacy for the arts and culture.

• *Connect with the schools.* Schools should strengthen arts education at all levels. Close connections with cultural institutions should be established.

• *Expand financial support.* Public and private funding sources should increase their financial support, giving special attention to emerging institutions.

• *Build networks.* Cultural institutions should work together, seeking collaboration to provide better service to the region.

• *Broaden the constituency.* Cultural institutions should respond aggressively to the diversity of the region and make a commitment to serve all populations more effectively.

• *Shape the future.* "Building community" should be the commitment of all cultural institutions as they work to implement the report's suggestions.

In closing, Myers noted that the Baltimore Area Community Foundation has committed $1 million to support the implementation of the report's recommendations.

SUMMARY OF REMARKS BY CHRIS ALLEN

Using the example of Arkansas Power and Light, Chris Allen offered ideas about how to attract money from new corporate partners. "My company's approach to giving has become increasingly focused during the past three years," Allen reported. As a regulated monopoly with "a captive audience," Arkansas Power and Light believes it has a corporate obligation to become involved in the economic and cultural development of the state. In 1992, the company donated more than $4 million for various projects.

Management decided some time ago to focus corporate giving in two major areas: education and job creation. In 1987, the company unveiled "Teamwork Arkansas," the state's largest single private sector initiative for economic development, earmarking between $10 million and $15 million over five years to create new and better-paying jobs. Teamwork planners have used this money to emphasize the importance of industrial recruitment, national and international advertising, and community development. Arkansas communities, by understanding these processes, can adequately respond to— and win over—industrial prospects looking to relocate to their areas.

"One of the most exciting funding ventures that we have been involved with is a community/cultural institution partnership," Allen said. The city of Helena joined with the Delta Cultural Center and its not-for-profit affiliate, the Delta Cultural Foundation, in an economic development program that includes creating a riverfront park along the Mississippi River. Issues addressed include the development of a downtown marketplace, downtown housing, and heritage tourism. "Early on, area leaders and members of the cultural center and foundation realized that outside help was needed for long-range planning and for building broad-based citizen involvement," Allen explained. Teamwork Arkansas helped enroll Helena and West Helena in a program, "Shaping North American Cities," run by Partners for Livable Places. A team of facilitators held community planning sessions, and working committees were formed to set goals in several areas: community development, housing renewal, development of downtown and the riverfront park, and assessment and promotion of community strength. "To our knowledge, the community has never come together like this to set economic development goals," said Allen.

With these efforts as a base, the Delta Cultural Center and Foundation were able to enlist other organizations: Southwestern Bell, utility companies, the Winthrop Rockefeller Foundation, and Shore Bank in Chicago among them. "It's wonderful how a chain reaction is set in motion when people get excited," Allen said. This excitement was a major reason for the American Institute of Architects' (AIA) selection of Helena as a site for its "Search for Shelter" program. AIA created a development plan, "Rebuild Helena," that includes affordable housing for low- and moderate-income people as well as landscaping and beautification. Currently, the riverfront and downtown marketplace development efforts have convinced a riverboat line to make Helena a stop on its routes, thereby providing an influx of tourists and tourist dollars.

In closing, Allen offered some tips for seeking funding for community/cultural institution partnerships:

• *Research the company.* "When you ask a corporation for money, it's like a job interview," Allen offered. "Get a copy of the annual report and some publications for employees, and see what the company's goals are. Craft your position paper or request to show that you are trying to reach goals that are in line with theirs."

• *Ask for seed money.* If the corporation does not know your organization well, this may be the best approach. "Show you are getting other organizations and corporations involved, and then go back to ask for a larger donation later," Allen advised. If a company can make a one-time contribution, "think endowment."

• *Ask for volunteer time from donors' employees.* "We are much more excited about giving to an organization that our people are involved with," Allen noted.

• *Ask for expertise.* Organizations can get professional help from donors and potential donors that they could not otherwise afford.

• *Show that your organization is watching costs.* "That goes over beautifully," Allen said. "Speak their language and show accountability."

• *Obtain contracts for large donations.* A contract is an important tool for spelling out plans and goals—"but make sure you can deliver what is promised."

SUMMARY OF REMARKS BY WARREN MERRICK

Warren Merrick began with a nod to the future, noting that based on predictions of changing demographics, economic obligations, and the need to be globally competitive, it is crucial "that we do not leave any people by the wayside, because we do not have many resources to waste." In recognition of that fact, Freedom Theatre, Pennsylvania's oldest African-American theatrical-performing arts facility, devotes a substantial portion of its energy to working with youth. According to Merrick, the theater trains more than 700 students each year; about 600 are young people. Of the students trained by the theater, 98 percent graduate from high school and 85 percent attend college. "That is significant," Merrick added, "because we are located in one of the most impoverished neighborhoods in Philadelphia."

Merrick offered some general considerations on forming partnerships with the public and private sectors. First, the prospective partners have to recognize a problem or need that the cultural institution can address. The next step is an analysis of the investment potential: Is the partnership a good risk? Finally, the institution has to be motivated to address the problem with its partners. Freedom Theatre, for example, has been successful in forming partnerships within the public sector. Merrick noted that Philadelphia has a strong group of elected African-American officials who recognize the service the theater provides. "We train actors, singers, and dancers, but we also humanize people," he explained. "We help them to improve their self-image, and that helps them succeed in many areas of life." Some have gone on to professional careers in television and theater, but many have chosen other careers.

In addition to its training ventures, Freedom Theatre produces a full season of plays each year. After the death of its founder, John Allen, the theater conducted a national search for a new artistic director. The new director, Walter Dallas, has put together an advisory team that will enable the theater to continue to develop artistically "I mention this because these things become selling points to the corporate community," Merrick noted. "A corporation wants to know what you are doing and what's in it for them." From the corporate perspective, Freedom Theatre's training programs make it a good investment. "We provide an alternative to the streets," Merrick said. He is sure, for instance, that one reason Philadelphia escaped rioting in the wake of the first Rodney King verdict is that the city has a strong infrastructure of cultural organizations that provide a direction and an outlet for inner-city youth.

Freedom Theatre has also formed a successful partnership that has helped Philadelphia attract numerous African-American conventions. Realizing the potential (the African-American hospitality industry in the United States generates $22 billion of income per year), members of the Coalition of African-American Cultural Organizations formed a committee that helped promote the city. About $90 million has been generated in African-American convention business since 1988. "Even before cultural pluralism became popular, we worked in concert with other organizations and institutions to see that we made Philadelphia a better place to live, work, and visit," Merrick said. Currently, Freedom Theatre is involved in the Avenue of the Arts project as the anchor for the northern segment of the proposed cultural district.

SUMMARY OF REMARKS BY WILLIAM BONDURANT

William Bondurant offered a lighthearted history of famous partnerships and the lessons learned from them—beginning with Adam, Eve, and the serpent. The moral to that story is: Partnerships can get into more trouble without the government's help than with it. Ancient partnerships involving governmental participation include the pyramids, the Colossus of Rhodes, and the Great Wall of China. Though monumental, "they were not built by volunteers from the private sector," said Bondurant. "The moral here is to build contemporary communities as well as tourist attractions." Skipping ahead to the partnerships forged with royalty by explorers such as Magellan and Columbus, Bondurant noted they often missed their targets by as much as 12,500 miles. The moral? It's okay for partners to change their course in mid-ocean.

Turning to contemporary times, Bondurant noted seriously that partnerships such as those established by local and national public radio and television are working well and involve the public, private, and independent sectors. "These are partnerships in the best tradition," he said. "The moral is that partnerships are the way to go."

The giving climate has chilled in the recent recession, and Bondurant noted several related statistics from a recent Gallup poll, reported in the December 1992 issue of the *Chronicle of Philanthropy.* Charitable giving by the average American household dropped by more than 19 percent between 1989 and 1991. Fewer households contributed in 1991 than in 1989, and volunteer time also decreased. However, the majority of Americans have not abandoned philanthropy. "Many, even without jobs, continue giving, although at a lower amount," Bondurant said. "That bears out the experience that even in a recession, generous givers give generously." The poll also found that nine out of ten people believe charities are needed more now than five years ago; three-fourths said charities play a major role in making communities better places to live.

It is not always easy to discern why people are willing to give, especially during an economic downturn. The desire to volunteer one's services seems to be a primary impetus, as evidenced by the fact that people whose households gave money but did not volunteer reported an average contribution of $477, while those who did volunteer contributed an average of $1,155. Income tax deductions may increase the size of the gift, though not the desire to make the gift in the first place. Religion also played a role. Two-thirds of the members of religious congregations gave to secular charities (compared to one-half of nonmembers). Perhaps most important, being asked to give was a critical element; people asked to give are more than twice as likely to do so as those who are not. Having positive giving experiences as a young person was also crucial; in fact, volunteering, giving or soliciting gifts, or participating in civic activities was the single most important predictor of an adult's giving patterns. The survey also found that young people, single people, and members of minority groups were the least likely to be asked to give money or attend a charity event, even though they are the ones who increased their giving and volunteering during the recession.

Compared with individuals, foundations have different issues to consider when giving. To illustrate this difference, Bondurant reviewed the experiences of the Mary

Reynolds Babcock Foundation in funding partnerships, from grants to the Boston and Washington children's museums to the Reynolda House Museum of American art in Winston-Salem. "I think we are typical of many smaller foundations," he noted. "We look at the local opportunities, and we also look regionally and nationally and try to do a lot of cross-pollinating." In screening applicants, the foundation asked what value was added by the partnership. "I think of many of these partnerships as value-added mergers," Bondurant explained. "We asked this question to avoid funding a new layer of bureaucracy between those who ultimately get the benefit and those who are doing the funding."

Other efforts have included the Parents as Teachers program, which helps parents learn how to become their child's first teacher. Several years ago, teachers, parents, corporations, and local school administrators in one North Carolina town formed a partnership to start education in the home before children reach school age. Their work soon captured the attention of the state Department of Public Instruction (DPI). A grant from the Babcock Foundation helped get the program started; its success has convinced the DPI to replicate it across North Carolina. "The enthusiasm of the local citizens, the timing of the effort, and the value added by each partner made this grant nearly undeniable by the foundation," Bondurant explained.

In discussing what foundations look for in making decisions about grants, Bondurant mentioned the "threshold question": Has the applicant looked at the foundation's guidelines? In making a successful approach to a foundation, Bondurant noted that a clear and compelling mission statement is important, as is evidence of an able board and staff. Resourcefulness, not just in getting foundation dollars but in getting in-kind contributions and volunteer help, shows a foundation that its money can be leveraged for greater impact.

Commitment and perseverance are crucial to winning a grant. "It frequently takes a year, or two or three, to position yourself with a foundation to be in the front of the line," Bondurant remarked. He also suggested playing capital and program grants off one another, saying to one foundation, "If we get money from the other for capital, will you give us program?" and doing the same at the other foundation. A realistic budget that shows the value of volunteer effort as well as out-of-pocket costs is necessary, as is proof of tax exemption.

"You can help foundations think beyond grantmaking," Bondurant said. "You can show them that just going for their dollars is not the noblest cause—that you are talking about something that goes beyond that." This might involve dealing with questions such as what role the foundation can play as a catalyst, perhaps by convening people at its location to help with the effort or by collaborating with others in the field.

QUESTIONS AND ANSWERS

Q: How can my organization obtain the funding and resources needed to develop a center of African-American art and culture? We, as a community organization, often do not have the expertise to do it alone.

Bondurant: Work on your mission statement, and give it that sense of urgency—the blue flame of need and impact. Broaden your base of supporters—not necessarily financial, but those who believe in the project—rather than have the project appear to be narrowly useful to just one segment of the community. Make it as appealing to as broad a population as possible. Check similar efforts in other cities to see what has worked. Begin locally with fund raising, but search nationally; national foundations will be more likely to be attentive if local sources have been forthcoming. You might ask some foundations for planning grants.

Q: We know that it takes a long time to build partnerships. How do you keep an organization's project alive with corporate funders over that long period of time?

Allen: Once a corporation has funded a small project, come back periodically and tell them about it. If something goes wrong, don't wait a year to let them know. Tell them what the problems are and how you are trying to alleviate them. Communication is the most important thing. Having a three- or four-year plan lets the corporation know you are looking ahead and using their dollars in an organized pattern.

Q: What about multiyear funding? How can we show a corporation that a project is worth that effort?

Bondurant: Some foundations prefer to fund start-up. They do that and then they get out. Other foundations want to fund that which is proven and established. My advice would be to determine which foundations are which and go to both groups. Tell the first group that if they will give you seed money you will begin working immediately with the second group. Tell the long-term group that you will come to them in a few years if the program works. Then go back to the first group and tell them the long-term funders have agreed to at least listen to you down the road.

Cultural Institutions and Communities: Partnerships for Economic Development

MODERATOR:

John Carter, President, Philadelphia Maritime Museum, Philadelphia

SPEAKERS:

Jeremy Alvarez, Executive Director, Central Philadelphia Development Corporation, Philadelphia

Ted Hershberg, Director, Center for Greater Philadelphia, Philadelphia

Helen Haynes, Executive Director, Coalition of African-American Cultural Organizations

Joan Baldridge, Director, Department of Arkansas Heritage, Little Rock

Carol Brown, President, Pittsburgh Cultural Trust, Pittsburgh

Richard Fleming, Chairman of the Board, Community Development Ventures, Inc., Denver

---

SUMMARY OF REMARKS BY JOHN CARTER
The city of Philadelphia is no stranger to the use of cultural institutions as bases for community economic development. John Carter described several such development projects under way or planned there. The most visible is the Avenue of the Arts (or South Broad Street Development Project), which involves a partnership of both public and private organizations. Another, the New Market Redevelopment Project, which has been privately funded for the most part, will extend the "cultural loop" that now encompasses the Center City District.

The Philadelphia Maritime Museum, which Carter

heads, is part of a project at Penn's Landing that will utilize the museum as a cultural anchor to spur further development of Penn's Landing along the lines of New York's South Street Seaport. Adding to the opportunities for visitors is the recently opened New Jersey Aquarium, linked by ferry to Penn's Landing. Carter predicted that "cultural agencies and organizations will be able to share in the boom created by these development projects in many ways, particularly if they can package and market their offerings to the crowds that the Center City District and a new convention center will create."

While that is good news, Carter admitted that cultural organizations have been hard-hit by the recent economic downturn, and many local organizations are barely hanging on. Thus, cultural organizations will most likely be forced to devise public and private partnerships "on a scale infrequently witnessed in the past." Carter predicted that public funding through bond issues as well as private funding through straight-line mortgages will become prevalent.

SUMMARY OF REMARKS BY JEREMY ALVAREZ

Alvarez's organization, the Central Philadelphia Development Corporation (CPDC), is a not-for-profit planning and development group. Alvarez prefaced his discussion of a CPDC project—the South Broad Street Development Project—with some general remarks on public-private partnerships. Economic might is no longer concentrated in urban centers. Investment in the suburbs and beyond has diffused the American economic system over the last two decades. Municipal competition for tax income and jobs is fierce. Furthermore, the current "recession" is more than it seems: Alvarez called it a "huge shake-out, where sloppy, inefficient, and unfocused organizations are dropping like old leaves."

The challenge for public-private partnerships is to find a strategic focus, a rationale. For urban policy makers, this means the identification of a clear marketing strategy, a "niche" that explains why cities are valuable.

For Alvarez, that niche is diversity. Cities "have to build on their differences. The very complexity that diverse people and activities create, that is the product."

Other assets that accrue to the cities include history, architecture, and cultural attractions. "Do you go to London or Paris to see their modern office complexes?" Alvarez asked. "You go for museums and theaters and the texture of old places." American cities, though younger than those of Europe, can offer the same things; suburbs cannot. With many marketing analyses indicating an increased demand for travel over the next few decades, cities have an opportunity to cash in on the trend. The central focus of the rationale, then, is that cultural attractions are critical to the success—and, indeed, the survival—of urban centers. Optimizing a city's cultural offerings should thus be a primary goal of urban economic development.

In discussing investment, Alvarez recalled the "heyday of urban renewal" when government funds were available to sustain initial losses to allow projects to reach full development. "While the concept is still alive, the money is gone," Alvarez noted. "Clinton is not going to be able to change this." Forging partnerships is now "the only way to go."

To forge successful partnerships, the leaders of both government and cultural institutions need to adjust their focus. Alvarez suggested several key changes for the latter:

• Understand the economic relationships between institutions and their surroundings.

• Look beyond internal budget problems and present hard data to governments, so the impact of the institution on the local economy is clear. "It's not enough to say, 'We're good for this area,'" Alvarez warned.

• Emphasize the public interest; synergetic relationships among all those groups involved with cultural institutions—government, funders, users, and so on—must be identified and nurtured.

• Study and improve user experience.

• Include outside support (restaurants, parking lots, hotels) as part of your institution's overall plan.

Alvarez outlined three bases for building successful partnerships with government:

1. *The project must have a demonstrable public benefit.* The two biggest components of public benefit are the creation of jobs and the revitalization of the community. "If the museum board is seen as the recipient of the grant, if it is seen as their project, outside support will deteriorate."

2. *Economic leverage is essential.* An institution must be able to show that money other than public dollars will be invested. The important question is: Can you bring new money to the table?

3. *There must be a specific return to the government.* To put it simply: Will the government make money on the deal?

All of these ideas and suggestions were put to use in the South Broad Street Development Project. As Alvarez described the process, it began with administrators consolidating ideas that were "already on the street" in regard to community development. Planners then used the resulting ideal development plan to drum up support from foundations, who funded more serious planning. That led to the project gaining support until government deemed it to be in the public interest. The process continued with more work demonstrating specific economic benefits, followed by a legislative proposal that resulted in about $70 million for the project. "But it is by no means a done deal," Alvarez noted. "There are still a lot of private dollars needed to meet the leverage goals."

SUMMARY OF REMARKS BY TED HERSHBERG

Speaking about regional arts and cultural initiatives, Ted Hershberg noted that the mission of the Center for Greater Philadelphia is "to get Philadelphia and the suburban communities that surround it to work together, because they share a common destiny." The premise behind such an initiative is that the city and surrounding counties could share a regional tax base to support cultural institutions.

Hershberg began by noting how important the hospitality industry is to Philadelphia. "The key question for Philadelphia is: Will people spend $50 on hot dogs and pretzels and then get on their way to New York or Atlantic City, or will they stay three or four nights, shop, eat, and spend $1,000?" The answer depends on downtown Philadelphia's ability to attract visitors.

Cultural institutions are an important part of the hospitality industry, but how can they use that position to gain funding? Though it has been done elsewhere (Hershberg mentioned Denver), "it's more of an art than a science to replicate past successes." So far, the Center for Greater Philadelphia has approached the issue in two ways: First, the center attempted to discover "how much money is out there" by asking the Pennsylvania Economy League to draw up a menu of revenue that could be raised from different taxes. Second, it has asked the Greater Philadelphia Cultural Alliance to determine the operating budgets of various arts and cultural groups in both the city and the suburbs. "The concept is very undefined," Hershberg said. "The idea is to provide a pot of money that can be shared across the city and suburban counties by all arts and cultural institutions." The most significant challenge is in defining what constitutes the region.

Hershberg believes that cities and suburbs must work together "or we will miss the boat in the regional economy." Cultural institutions can make the argument that they contribute to economic development either directly or indirectly (through adding to a city's quality of life). And they can also make the argument that, as Hershberg put it, "if you can get people in the city and suburbs to buy into something nonthreatening, such as sharing the arts and culture, then maybe they can begin to consider other issues of mutual concern further down the road."

In southeastern Pennsylvania, county and local governments are overwhelmingly dependent on real estate taxes for revenue and often fall short of their revenue goals. A movement is under way among them to shift from real estate to sales and personal income taxes. Hershberg sees an opportunity here for cultural institutions to help business and civic leaders by asking state legislators to shift revenue-raising authority to local levels, where it is badly needed. State officials, he noted, have not been forthcoming in giving local governments access to those revenues. Institutions that could participate in this reorientation of resources would be in an excellent position to engage in "a little quid pro quo." This, said Hershberg, could open up significant new sources of funding while reestablishing the central role of cultural institutions in the community.

SUMMARY OF REMARKS BY HELEN HAYNES

Helen Haynes discussed the effect of community-based organizations, especially multicultural and minority-based organizations, on economic development. She pointed out, as an example, that one of the main incentives for additional funding for Philadelphia's Avenue of the Arts was a $60 million legislative initiative; the chair of the appropriations committee required the money to be linked to development on North Broad Street, in the African-American community.

"Black cultural institutions are the vehicle for transmission of the contribution and traditions of African Americans," Haynes stated, adding that the impact of federal and municipal redevelopment programs on older black communities needs to be assessed. Often these communities are in or near city centers. Because these communities are a "major connective muscle" between black culture and black residential space, Haynes suggested "carefully reexamining the relationships between

institutions and cultural organizations that have helped to nurture the African-American sense of identity and the consequences of the dispersal and loss of these institutions." Public support for community-based cultural institutions should not be thought of as subsidies, but as crucial investments for rebuilding.

Haynes listed some of the ways that African-American cultural institutions play important roles in their communities: They help preserve culture; contribute to local economies by employing African-American artists, administrators, and technicians; purchase goods and services from local businesses; train young people; and contribute to neighborhood revitalization through institutional ownership, property renovation, and development of housing.

The Philadelphia-based Coalition of African-American Cultural Organizations is an eighteen-member consortium encompassing a variety of disciplines, from dance to literature. All are community-based organizations that serve neighborhoods, while also attracting audiences from all parts of the city (some even attract national and international audiences through touring). Most work directly with public schools, neighborhood centers, and other social service organizations, "helping fill the gaps in these agencies that budget cuts have left." In 1991, the cumulative budgets of the member organizations totaled more than $5.3 million; more than half have budgets under $75,000 per year. As a consequence, most of the budgets are spent directly on services to the community. Member organizations employ more than 400 artists, administrators, and technicians on a full- or part-time basis. "When we start to define economic impact, we have to think about how it affects these communities," Haynes asserted. "How many people are being employed? How is this money being spent? How does it affect the general well-being of the community?"

Black cultural institutions have played a major role in urban development by providing neighborhood identity and cohesion—two keys to urban revitalization. They also assist in training unemployed or underemployed residents. The most striking example of this is Freedom Theatre, which was contracted by the McDonald's fast food restaurant chain to provide a training program to enhance the customer service of the company's employees. Using arts and culture, Freedom Theatre is known for training young people, "helping them to refocus on a positive identity, to have a different attitude toward themselves and thus other people." Freedom Theatre, said Haynes, fills the need for nurturance and support, particularly among youth, which is important to emotional well-being and mental health. Likewise, the theater assists in local childhood education, enhancing for children the building of basic skills, literacy, communication, and discipline.

The coalition has played a major role in helping Philadelphia gain recognition by the U.S. Department of Commerce as the city most visited by African-American tourists. As a member of the Convention and Visitors Bureau, the coalition participates in entertaining meeting planners and journalists. "We help sell the city to these professionals and tourists," said Haynes. Now, the Coalition is looking at ways to continue attracting people to its institutions, using better marketing, audience development, and education.

SUMMARY OF REMARKS BY JOAN BALDRIDGE

To illustrate the interrelatedness of museums and communities, Joan Baldridge related the story of the Delta Cultural Center, a state-owned facility in Helena, Arkansas. State and local planners opened the center in October 1990 with two express purposes in mind: to present the diverse culture of the Mississippi Delta and to assist in the economic recovery of the region.

The center grew out of an annual blues festival, begun in 1986, which regularly drew large crowds to Helena. The manager of Main Street Helena, the festival's sponsoring organization, wanted to find a way to incorporate an old railway depot donated by the city into the festival, perhaps as a performance stage. Joined by the state representative and mayor, the manager sought funding from then-governor Bill Clinton. Clinton suggested that Helena go further to create something that "would showcase the diverse culture of the Delta while also developing the economy."

Baldridge's job was to make that vision a reality. A planning committee of representatives from the Department of Arkansas Heritage, the state arts council, the state historic preservation program, and the director of the Old State House joined with others from the governor's office to bring the center to life. "I wish I could tell you our meetings were smooth and free from anguish," Baldridge said. "We struggled, however, with concept, mission, programming, and administrative structure issues." In addition, larger dilemmas had to be faced; the most prominent, perhaps, being how to bring people together across racial and class lines to concentrate on presenting the Delta's diverse heritage. It was, Baldridge noted, "a daunting task, and one that must be ongoing."

A large ad hoc advisory committee strove to be as inclusive as possible. "We told people to invite anyone who was interested," Baldridge recalled. She also met with smaller groups, such as the biracial committee of the Greater Helena Chamber of Commerce. The committee was "very suspicious of the concept of the center," she said. "But by the time the meeting was over, I think the group was just beginning to see that racial harmony could be the route to economic gain, and not just for whites." A multicultural perspective "was an absolutely critical element in forging the public-private partnership to develop this institution as an anchor for economic development," Baldridge noted.

In addition, the attitude of the community as a whole made an impact on the project. Baldridge spoke of the "underlying disbelief that anything would ever come out of all this talk." Some perceived the state government as the "knight in shining armor," come to rescue Helena from the dragon of economic woes. Indeed, legislative support was crucial, and Baldridge noted that she "could not imagine taking on this kind of project without that kind of help." But she also admitted that the enthusiasm for the project has never developed into the full public-private partnership that planners originally hoped for. "Sometimes, when I go to Helena, I have the feeling that people think I must have a check for them."

The center's economic impact has been mixed. "I am sad to say that it is still Helena's museum," Baldridge said. "The rest of the Delta does not realize the potential impact of the center." Visitation figures have not reached original expectations, due to a lack of advertising dollars. Nor has the amount of private investment in Helena lived up to projections. But the center has contributed to an influx of tourists linked to the two riverboats that stop in town. It is hoped that an increase in private investment in tourism-related businesses will result from the traffic generated by the riverboats and the center. "I don't think there is any doubt that the economic well-being of the community is dependent on tourism stimulated by a cultural facility," Baldridge concluded.

SUMMARY OF REMARKS BY CAROL BROWN

The Pittsburgh Cultural Trust, which Carol Brown heads, was established in 1984 as a public-private partnership to oversee the development of a cultural district in downtown Pittsburgh. It was, Brown explained, planned very much as a "cultural and arts development agency."

The trust's mission is simple: "Improve the quality of life in Pittsburgh by developing performing and visual arts facilities in a formerly ruined fourteen-square-block downtown area." As with many such developmental projects, the increased number of visitors to the area, who come to partake of the cultural offerings, has been the impetus for economic and commercial development. The unique aspect of the Pittsburgh Trust, however, is that it receives a portion of the cash flow from the commercial development around the cultural and arts facilities it has developed.

In the early 1980s, this fourteen-block area was, in effect, a red-light district that had missed the redevelopment taking place elsewhere downtown. During its first ten years, the trust put together a total investment package of $210 million from the public and private sectors. The second ten-year plan calls for about $512 million, including $390 million in commercial investment.

The plan for the district focused on three major issues: buying up property, establishing arts and entertainment facilities to attract commercial development, and developing other amenities, such as parks. The trust's board was formed specifically to renovate and restore an old movie palace, which became the Benedum Center for the Arts. (It joined the Pittsburgh Symphony's Heinz Hall, the only similar facility already located in the area.) With $24 million from federal grants and city and county bond issues and $18 million from the private sector, including a lead gift from a major foundation, the project was "a perfect example of a public-private partnership," said Brown. Next, the trust bought an old, more intimate vaudeville theater to attract small and mid-size arts organizations to the area. The theaters charge a "Robin Hood rental rate"—higher fees for commercial users and sliding scale fees for smaller organizations, based on the size of their operating budgets.

The trust is currently involved in building a Michael Graves-designed mixed-use facility to house the Pittsburgh Public Theater—another "classic example of a public-private partnership and the use of the arts to attract commercial development, with that development providing a cash flow back to the arts." When an office building and parking garage are completed, the ground rent payments will go to support four theaters in the district. "But the Trust's work is far from complete," noted Brown. It is working to attract galleries to the district and is planning streetscaping improvement. It also hopes to develop a riverfront park next year.

The economic benefits have been substantial. Since the trust began, three large office complexes have been built adjacent to the theaters, providing tax benefits to the city and county. Performances are up from 260 to 535 per year. And two of the last three years have seen more than 1 million people visit the district—all of them, of course, adding to the area's income.

Funders are often skeptical of such positive change. Thus, the trust engages the Pennsylvania Economy League to determine what changes have occurred to give a solid basis to its claims. A major study of the arts has also provided valuable data. For instance, 25 percent of the downtown audience for arts events comes from the city, 50 percent from the county, and 25 percent from the surrounding region, giving proof that the arts are a regional asset. As a result, the trust has launched a cultural tourism program aimed at West Virginia and eastern Ohio. Employment numbers provide proof of economic impact as well: The district's arts organizations and facilities now have a combined payroll of more than $19 million and provide jobs for 1,800 people.

Another benefit has been an increase in real estate tax revenues: up from $7 million in 1986 to $14.5 million in 1990. And the trust projects a $25 million figure by the year 2000. There are indirect benefits, too. Brown mentioned that the trust is working closely with community groups to ensure that its facilities are accessible to everyone. This strong economic showing has allowed the trust to benefit others: In the last five years, it has distributed more than $9 million worth of free tickets to underserved populations.

SUMMARY OF REMARKS BY RICHARD FLEMING

Richard Fleming described Denver's efforts to invest in cultural institutions as part of an overall strategy to turn around a sick economy. "We went through the triple whammy of the energy bust, the worldwide collapse of the semiconductor industry, and the decline of the agricultural industry," he recalled. We have the nation's worst vacancy rates in office, industrial, and residential property. We have had our highest unemployment rates in sixteen years. It may have been counterintuitive to suggest leading with a regional tax for cultural facilities, but that is what we did."

An economic study demonstrated that museums and other cultural institutions pump more money into the Colorado economy than many state attractions, including the Denver Broncos football team and the Vail ski resort. Given those numbers, the challenge for Denver developers was to use those institutions to create jobs and boost the economy. Through a series of legislative battles and a public referendum, the Cultural Facilities District was established, along with economic investment strategies that included the building of a new airport, a new convention center, a new baseball stadium, a new library, and completion of the Denver Arts Complex.

The Cultural Facilities District idea was born when a bill was introduced into the Colorado legislature that would have permitted the formation of arts tax districts statewide. These tax districts would provide funds for the creation and maintenance of arts organizations that would boost the state's economy. Though the original bill failed, a more organized attempt was made by four of the state's leading cultural institutions and spearheaded by a "wealthy, politically adroit" business executive and philanthropist. This bill called for a sales tax of one-tenth of a cent on the dollar to be used to fund these four institutions. When seven other institutions then tried to amend the bill to include themselves, a compromise was developed. Funds from the tax would be disbursed according to a three-tiered structure: tier one provided for older, more established institutions, tier two for institutions throughout the six-county Denver metro area, and tier three for emerging and grassroots organizations. When put to a public test, the measure was overwhelmingly approved, with 75 percent of the voters affirming the measure, even "in the middle of the worst economy in fifty years."

Those guiding the bill through the legislative process saw two strategic necessities early on: "Getting the voters to pass any tax increase was going to require the absolute support of the directors and trustees of all the institutions. And it was going to cost a lot of money." Convincing the various cultural institutions to present a united front was not an easy task. Fleming called it "the arts and culture equivalent of a disarmament agreement." In achieving cooperation among themselves, however, "they learned the value of ongoing and honest communication, not only with the electorate but among themselves."

Fleming noted the four main ingredients for a successful legislative initiative: First, there must be a champion—a powerful and recognizable person who is willing to lobby for the idea. Second, planners must have a volunteer corps willing to do the necessary work. These volunteers should be drawn from the participating institutions and guided by the boards of trustees (a staff-driven initiative would likely not be seen as having a broad base of support). Third, budgets must be planned. Each institution must provide a pragmatic projection of what it needs and how much it will take to get the initiative passed. Fourth, success depends on a competent campaign manager. "Hire him or her early and follow his or her advice absolutely," Fleming advised.

Fleming also reminded participants that "this is not about changing people's attitudes toward quality of life. It has to do with economic development, education, or whatever is the most important community value at the time of the election." Such a statement may sound cynical, but as Fleming pointed out, voters must perceive the arts to be as important to their community as public safety or the sewer system. "They need to believe that without a healthy arts community, they will not have a healthy, thriving city," he said.

Finally, Fleming remarked that "lest you think we in Colorado have got funding of the arts solved," the last statewide election saw the passage of a radical tax and spending limitation amendment. The cultural initiative will thus have to face reauthorization in 1996.

Conference Summary

SPEAKERS:

Harold K. Skramstad Jr., President, Henry Ford Museum and Greenfield Village, Dearborn, Michigan

Sister Mary Scullion, Project Home, Philadelphia

SUMMARY OF REMARKS BY HAROLD SKRAMSTAD

Harold Skramstad indicated that the language of the conference—which focused on issues such as partnership, bargaining, inclusion, trust, risk, failure, entrepreneurship, mutual self-interest, listening, added value, passion, and commitment—had been quite different from that used at most traditional museum meetings, which is a fault, he concluded, "of the museum community." Discussing and enacting these issues implies a base of "equality," he maintained, which is the key to successful partnerships of any kind. They also have "political dimensions": equal people coming together to discover mutual ground for accomplishing common good. In addition, there is an emphasis on a larger vision of society: "not what we can do for ourselves, but what we can do for others."

Skramstad stated that *Excellence and Equity: Education and the Public Dimension of Museums,* published by the American Association of Museums, is a significant policy document because it clarifies the mission of contemporary museums as being fundamentally educational institutions. In light of the failure of traditional educational establishments to offer a "context and authenticity that provide the best learning experience," Skramstad declared, museums can play a critical role.

There has been a "revival of museums as care-giving institutions," he continued, "which is our most traditional role." People who have perceived the museum in that capacity have "understood the code" and have "drawn out the care" of the museum. Some people, however, have not understood the code and have been excluded. Thus, a more inclusive role for museums calls for "new messages, a new vocabulary, and a new authenticity that can engage a broader public."

In closing, Skramstad outlined ten "charges for action" for museums:

1. Understand the mission of the institution. Mission statements must define the goals of an organization, the expected outcome of those goals, and the value of that outcome for society.

2. Develop ways to measure the success of an organization, both quantitatively and qualitatively. When institutions interact with partners and other strategic alliances, such as the political, corporate, or foundation communities, those groups want to know how to assess the results and added value. In addition, the measurement of success validates the financial support of institutions.

3. Be honest about mistakes. Often, institutions need the help of communities to identify and understand their mistakes.

4. Recognize the limits of available resources, but "stretch" them for their maximum benefit.

5. Admit that change has consequences. There will be "risk and disruption as well as unhappy people, unhappy communities, and unhappy partners," but change is necessary.

6. Realize that institutions cannot deal with diversity "outside" their organizations unless it is a vital part of their "organizational life."

7. Recognize that "community" denotes a broad range of components, from the people who live in the service area of a museum to the other "legitimate parts," such as the political leadership, the corporate leadership, and the "visionary members." Alliances and partnerships across the broadest range of the community have driven the revival of education and of the economic and social life of many cities.

8. Use mentors rather than replicate model programs. Each museum must establish its identity by discovering community members with insight, enthusiasm, compassion, commitment, and vision and by absorbing their assistance and resources.

9. Develop new metaphors for museums. The traditional metaphors of the museum as "teacher, scholar, and repository" must be replaced with the expanded vision of institutions and communities. The new metaphors must "reenergize" the museum as "listener, mentor, broker, care-giver, mediator, and forum."

10. Search for the common elements that bind, rather than divide, institutions and communities and that create successful and "whole" human beings. Arts and cultural institutions must claim their central role in the development of productive communities.

SUMMARY OF REMARKS BY SISTER MARY SCULLION

"To save our world from destruction," Sister Mary Scullion asserted, museums and other cultural institutions must aggressively address the problems in our cities. Intrinsic to that challenge is the cultivation of the arts and culture because they "make us who we are and express our truth." It is impossible to "separate life and art," she maintained. Thus, the arts and cultural community must address the poverty that affects two-thirds of the people in the world; must help to heal the addiction, abuse, and disease that kill our "brothers and sisters"; and must "shine forth with knowledge and education" to combat widespread illiteracy.

Philadelphia, she noted, is an inspiring example of how arts and cultural organizations can transform the "social and economic life of a city." Institutions like the Free Library, the Franklin Institute, the Please Touch Museum, and the Afro-American Historical and Cultural Museum have "addressed urban problems and have shed light on their resolution."

Scullion believes that "the world will be saved by beauty," as Dostoyevski wrote. And she left conference attendees with the assurance that their vision represents the "hope for our world."